Amazing Rain Forest

RAIN FORESTS TODAY

Ted O'Hare

*Mist lies above the green hills
of a Central American rain forest.*

Rourke

Publishing LLC
Vero Beach, Florida 32964

www.rourkepublishing.com

PHOTO CREDITS: All photos © Lynn M. Stone except cover and page 8 (both), 15, 21 (main) ©James H. Carmichael

Editor: Frank Sloan

Cover and page design by Nicola Stratford

Library of Congress Cataloging-in-Publication Data

O'Hare, Ted, 1961-
  Amazing rain forest / Ted O'Hare.
     p. cm. -- (Rain forests today)
  Includes bibliographical references and index.
  ISBN 1-59515-151-6 (hardcover)
  1. Rain forests--Juvenile literature. I. Title. II. Series: O'Hare, Ted, 1961-   Rain
forests today.
  QH86.O39 2004
  577.34--dc22
                                                                    200401076

Printed in the USA

CG/CG

Table of Contents

The cotton-top tamarin is an endangered animal living in Central and South America.

Amazing!

The world's tropical rain forests are truly amazing. They are amazingly green, wet, and wild. They are also amazingly rich in plant and animal life. About one half of the **species**, or kinds, of plants and animals of the world are found in tropical rain forests.

Tropical rain forests cover about 6 to 7 percent of the world's land surface.

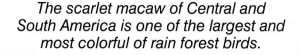

The scarlet macaw of Central and South America is one of the largest and most colorful of rain forest birds.

Tropical Rain Forest Regions

The world's tropical region is also called the "tropics." This area roughly follows the equator. The **equator** is an imaginary line around the middle of the earth.

Tropical rain forests grow where the average monthly temperature is about 75 degrees Fahrenheit (24 degrees C.) or more.

Most rain forests have about 80 inches (200 cm) of rain each year.

Warm and wet, rain forests have developed along the equator.

Rain forest fills the Napo River valley in eastern Ecuador.

Rain Forests around the World

The largest tropical rain forest is in northeastern South America. Brazil alone has about a third of the world's tropical rain forests.

Other large rain forests are in Southeast Asia and West Africa. Smaller rain forests are in Central America, southern Mexico, northeastern Australia, and on some Caribbean and South Pacific islands.

San Fernando Falls gushes into the tropical rain forest in eastern Costa Rica.

The Rain Forest Canopy

Rain forests are jungles of ferns, leaves, vines, trees, and bushes. They stay green all year round.

All tropical rain forests grow in "layers." The top layer is the roof of the forest. It is known as the **canopy**. A few tall trees even grow above the canopy.

Air plants crowd the branches of a tree poking above the rain forest "canopy."

Below the Canopy

The **understory** lies beneath the canopy. This part of the rain forest is made up of palms, small trees, and other plants.

The forest floor is at the bottom. The plants there are not thick. This is because so little sunlight reaches it. Without sunlight, green plants cannot grow well.

Leaves and branches of the canopy block sunlight to the understory and forest floor.

Welfia palms grow in the jungle understory.

Toads live on and under the rain forest floor.

Inside the Rain Forest

The air in a tropical rain forest is warm and humid. It is filled with moisture. The average temperature changes very little.

In most tropical rain forests there are about 200 rainy days a year. But some rain forests also have dry periods.

A red-eyed treefrog takes shelter from the rain.

Plants of the Rain Forest

Rain forest plants are well watered and well fed. Many of them grow all year long. The roots of plants quickly take **nutrients** from the soil. If they didn't, rain would carry these nutrients deep into the ground.

Mosses, vines, flowers, trees, and **epiphytes** are just a few of the plants that grow in the rain forests.

This long-leaved epiphyte is a type of bromeliad.

The bright colors of poison arrow frogs may help keep predators away.

Animals of the Rain Forest

Animals can be found in the leaf litter on the floor of the forest and also in the tops of the tallest trees. Insects of all shapes and sizes live in the forests. So do brightly colored birds, along with snakes and lizards, frogs and toads, and mammals.

Scientists have identified thousands of species of plants and animals. Thousands more still wait to be discovered and studied.

Clouded leopards live in a few of the Asian rain forests.

Discoveries in the Rain Forest

Long ago people found uses for plants growing in the rain forests. Almost a hundred rain forest plants are being used to make medicines. Scientists are studying even more plants for possible use as medicines.

Scientists look for helpful plants in a South American rain forest.

Rain Forests in Danger

More and more tropical rain forests are being cut down to create land for building and farming. This destruction threatens the **habitats** of rain forest plants, animals, and people. It is likely that many species of plants and animals will soon become **extinct**.

The destruction of rain forests is a problem in many countries.

Glossary

canopy (KAN uh pee) — the "roof" of upper branches and leaves in a forest

epiphytes (EHP uh fites) — any of several kinds of plants that grow on other plants, without harming the host plants

equator (ee KWAY tur) — the line drawn on maps around the earth's middle

extinct (EK stinkt) — no longer existing

habitats (HAB uh tatz) — special areas in which plants and animals live

nutrients (NU tree untz) — any of several "good" substances needed for health and growth

species (SPEE sheez) — a certain kind of plant or animal within a closely related group

understory (UN der stor ee) — the layer of small trees below the forest canopy

23

Index

Further Reading

Castner, James L. *Deep in the Amazon.* Six volumes. Benchmark Books, 2001-2002.
Chinery, Michael. *Secrets of the Rainforest.* Six volumes. Crabtree, 2000-2001.
Rain Forests of the World. Eleven volumes. Marshall Cavendish, 2002.

Websites to Visit

www.enchantedlearning.com/subjects/rainforest/
www.rainforest-alliance.org/kids_teachers/index.html
www.junglephotos.com/
www.ran.org/info_center/teacherstudent.html
www.rainforesteducation.com

About the Author

Ted O'Hare is an author and editor of children's nonfiction books. He divides his time between New York City and a home upstate.